BUT WAIT! ...
THERE'S MORE

A Book of Inspirational Christian Poetry

Ann Zwemer

Also by Ann Zwemer

Professional Adjustments and Ethics for Nurses in India (seven editions)

Basic Psychology for Nurses in India (two editions)

Just a Moment (two editions)

Longings

Z's Reflections

BUT WAIT! ... THERE'S MORE

A Book of Inspirational Christian Poetry

Ann Zwemer

WestBow Press books may be ordered through booksellers or by contacting:

WestBow Press
A Division of Thomas Nelson & Zondervan
1663 Liberty Drive
Bloomington, IN 47403
www.westbowpress.com
1 (866) 928-1240

ISBN: 978-1-9736-2841-5 (sc)
ISBN: 978-1-9736-2842-2 (e)

Library of Congress Control Number: 2018905676

Print information available on the last page.

WestBow Press rev. date: 5/11/2018

To
Christians
around the world

Contents

More Reflections by Ann Zwemer

Note that "R" = "Reflection"

Preface

As I wrote this after my eighty-fifth birthday in 2013, I heard announced that we now had sixty-two people in the world who are 110 years or older. So I assumed I may well have time to write another book.

This was a new and exciting territory for me and my family. I had never been at this age before! What does one do at this age? What can one do? What should one do and what should one not do? I'm eager to learn and experience whatever I can.

So I invite you to join me on this new journey.

Ann Zwemer

Acknowledgments

Many of my readers have encouraged me to continue writing even though my writing is neither voluminous nor conventional. I have chosen subjects that to me are extremely important and are truly matters of the heart. My thoughts are more than personal opinions; they are reflections of personal experiences.

I have received the greatest encouragement and personal assistance with the development of *But Wait! ... There's More* from my best friend, Llona (LaNay) Kitzing. She has worked with the most intense creativity as we read through each thought, poem, and reflection.

I am also grateful for Doug Saito, who provided me with the technological assistance I needed to produce this book electronically. Doug also assisted me in my communication with the publisher. In essence, he helped to make the publishing of *But Wait! ... There's More* possible.

But Wait! ... There's More

But wait ... there's more.
Sounds like
a promise
of something bigger,
something better.
There's more
of what?

Longevity
gives us
something more—
more time.

We are challenged
by what to do
with this time.

More time
to think,
to love,
to work,
to play,
to pray,
to do whatever
we can do
with this
gift of time,
this tiny
piece of eternity.

My Journey with God

I was aware
of God
during my
early years
as a part of
my family culture.
Because others
believed,
I believed.

As I matured,
I thought of God
as a father figure,
with authority
and love,
and eventually
including
mercy and
forgiveness.

Then, I met Jesus,
Son of God,
Son of Man.
Jesus,
Lord of my life,
keeper of my soul
as long as I live
and beyond
into eternity.

R1

If I could choose
any gift to give
my children
and grandchildren,
it would be
my Christian faith.

R2

In Jesus Christ,
I am
the light
of the world,
the salt
of the earth.

R3

The peace of God
cannot
be earned;
it is
a gift.

My Journey with Age

When I was very young,
age was very
attractive to me.
Each year
seemed a delight
that I eagerly embraced
as I added to my
physical stature and
developed
my thinking.

My adolescent
years seemed
to drag,
age so powerfully
beckoning me
toward adulthood
with its symbol
of freedom.

In midlife
my attitude
toward age
changed
unexpectedly
when I tried
to hide
its effects
on my body.

Not so with
my spirit.
My spirit
defies age,
becomes stronger
with time,
as long as
I walk closely
with the
Spirit of God.

R4

I will
accept
and
forgive
my
forgetfulness.

R5

I no longer
feel guilty
when I
take a nap
rather than
take a walk.

R6

When I walk,
a mile
seems
far longer
than
a mile.

R7

I will
accept
my shrinking
world
when
that time comes.

Don't Tell the Children

As a child,
when I did
something foolish,
I did not
tell my parents
unless
it was necessary.

Now,
as a parent,
I do not tell
my children
everything,
especially when
I do something
foolish.

Then,
with a
knowing smile,
I keep my
silence.

Reflections of a Patient

When I suddenly
become
a patient,
my entire life
changes
from
being a giver
to being
a receiver,
from
being fiercely
independent
to being helplessly
dependent,
from
giving commands
to being commanded,
from
meditating deeply
to thinking only
essential thoughts,
from
dressing with pride
to losing
all sense of dignity.

What a wonder then,
even in this
condition,
that I can still share
the love of God
with those
who care for me!

My Journey with Pain

I expect pain
to come to me
at some point
in my life.

Some pain
comes and goes;
some pain
comes and stays!
When pain stays,
it becomes
suffering.

When this happens
I want to
suffer well;
to suffer well
is a great
achievement.

Right now,
I don't know
how to
suffer well.
I do know
that when that
time comes,
as long as
I stay in touch
with Jesus,
I will know how.

To Suffer Well

To suffer well,
without complaint,
is a statement
of my faith
to the world
around me.

I begin when
I accept suffering
as a natural
part of life and
then move on
to a spiritual level
that is higher than
my physical and
emotional needs
and is given to me
by the grace and power
of Jesus Christ.

I suffer well
to glorify God,
help others,
and help myself.

R8

My illness
is only
a small part
of me.

R9

Sometimes
God just
wants me
to come
and *be*.

R10

It is
never too late
to forgive
another
person!

R11

I can
never
give away
too much
love.

Am I Healing or Wounding?

Every time
I interact
with
another person,
I am either
healing or
wounding
that person.

The longer I live,
the more
I want to be
a healer
rather than
a wounder.

To be a healer
I need
the power
of the Spirit
within me
to create
healing thoughts,
actions,
and words.

R12

The only Christ
others may see
is the Christ
they see
in me.

R13

Let the day
of my anger
be the day
of my
reconciliation!

R14

Sharing a smile
with others
while hurting
on the inside
is a special gift.

R15

A smile
transcends
all
language
barriers.

The Winds of Change

At first
I hardly
feel them,
like soft
gentle breezes
touching lightly
on my skin.
I feel more deeply
from within
when they tell
of things to come,
of different things
from those I now know.

When gentle breezes
become like winds and
blow more harshly,
showing me things
I may not like,
things affecting
my life's journey,
I know for sure
these are
the winds of change.

Making That Change, That Transition

Many an
ordinary move—
from rising
in the morning
to going
to bed at night—
is a change,
a transition
I make with
little or no effort.

I am
more challenged
by daily
in-between
changes
forcing me
to move
from one thing
to another
whether I'm
ready or not.

These changes
demand
a special discipline
that helps me take
the first step
in the new direction.
Then,
I'm on my way!

Taking That First Step

I cannot remember
my very first step
as a one-year-old.
I do know
that step opened up
a whole new world
to me.

The first step
of anything
is a new beginning
of something.
Something good?
Something
not so good?
Something bad?
It's my choice!

Wrestling with Fear

Fears assail me
both routinely
and unexpectedly
in many corners
of my life.

Little fears
allow me
to crush
and dismiss them.

Bigger,
more powerful
fears
give me
anxiety,
a racing heart,
physical
trepidation.

No matter the fear,
big or little,
with faith
I know I can
overcome it
if
I face it.

R16

Education is not
guaranteed
to produce
a better person.
It will produce
a different person.

R17

Being punctual
shows
respect
for the time
of other people.

R18

There are
always
clouds
in a
beautiful sky.

When Good Friends Die

Sometimes
I know it's coming;
sometimes
it's a shock
to learn
I've lost
a good friend.

When a good friend
passes
from this life
to the next,
I pause,
almost gasping
with the painful wrench
it gives
my body and soul.

It's like an
emotional and
spiritual wound
that needs healing,
which I find
in fellowship
with others and
in prayer
with God.

Letting Go

Life is full
of letting go
in myriad ways,
from the physical
to the emotional
and the spiritual.
Sometimes I choose
to let go
of something
or someone;
sometimes life
chooses for me.

Wisdom tells me
when it is time
to let go.

I let go
more easily
when I know
I cannot fall.
Faith will hold me
like a safety net
made up of the
presence of God.
The deeper
my faith,
the more easily
I can let go.

Filling My Emptiness

Throughout life
some form of loss
visits me
regularly,
creating fluctuating
senses of
emptiness
I must fill.

The choice
I make
each time
I fill
this emptiness
determines
the direction
of my life's
journey,
even to its
very end.

R19

I need to do
what I can do,
while accepting
what
I cannot do.

R20

One of life's
greatest assets
at any age
is
a good teacher.

R21

Material
possessions
gradually
lose value
to me
as I age.

R22

Letting go of
material possessions
gives me
a new sense
of freedom.

Leftover Time

Leftover time
comes to me
when I am early
or others are late.
It is an
unexpected
little gift of time.
The more
handicapped
I become,
the more
leftover time I have.
I need to choose
what to do
with this time.
Whatever I choose—
from exercise,
to music,
to meditation,
to prayer—
it should
enrich my life.

Contentment Enshrined

Contentment is
a holy,
blessed
condition of
mind and soul.
It is
different from
joy
or happiness.

Joy comes
when
happiness reaches
a peak.
Contentment
is the foundation
of happiness.

While
I eagerly embrace
joy and
happiness,
I deeply
treasure
contentment.

I know
I am truly
blessed
when I am
content.

R23

What I do or
what I have
is not
who I am.
Do I know
the difference?

R24

A good
sense of humor
can relieve
much
of life's pain.

My Spiritual Farewell

When I am gone
from this life,
it is just
the beginning
of my eternal life.

Fears and worries,
aches and pains,
will be no more,
for I will
be at peace
with Jesus.

My greatest wish
for you,
my loved ones
and my friends,
is that you live
your lives *now*
to the fullest,
until you, too,
make this transition
and join me here,
in this place.

More Reflections by Ann Zwemer

R25

I give
to God
by
giving
to people.

R26

The more
things
I have,
the more
problems
I have.

R27

God always
answers
my prayers,
though
it may not be
what I desire.

R28

As my choices
in life
multiply,
my priorities
must become
wiser.

R29

I am fully
mature
when I accept
responsibility
for
everything I do.

R30

The peace
of God
is a gift,
not something
I can earn.

R31

Everything
I see, hear,
and read
will become
me.

R32

All
world religions
seek God.
Only Christianity
seeks God
through
Jesus Christ.

R33

The only
time
I truly own
is
now.

R34

As I age,
my mind
always seems
to move faster
than
my body.

R35

Whatever I do,
wherever I go
today,
God is my
unseen guest.

R36

I seem to
get into debt
so easily.
Getting out of it
can be
more difficult.

R37

Take five!
Even
a short break
will help me
finish a
difficult task.

R38

I may have
many material
blessings:
without faith
I still live
in poverty.

R39

Symbols I use
every day
remind me
and the world
of
who I am.

R40

The more
faith
I give away,
the more
I will have.

About the Author

Ann Zwemer, BA, RN, MSC, is a published author of poetry, prose, and educational nursing texts. She spent eight years in India with her family as a missionary nurse for the Reformed Church in America. For the past sixteen years, she has attended the Braille Institute in San Diego and served as a volunteer teacher. She lives in California.

Printed in the United States
By Bookmasters